BUSY BUILDERS

AIRPORT

CONTENTS

ARRIVING AT THE AIRPORT

Airports are exciting places! All sorts of people pass through airports: pilots, crew members, and other travelers like you. Let's start your adventure by stepping inside the terminal building.

what's inside?

When you enter the terminal, you can see baggage check-in counters, electronic information boards, shops, and restaurants.

DEPARTURES

TIME	TO	FLIGHT	GATE	REMARKS
7:35	PARIS	CD1147	A2	ON TIME
7:40	HONG KONG	AN0341	B5	ON TIME
7:45	BARCELONA	PA7635	A1	ON TIME
7:55	NEW YORK	NY1730	C1	DELAYED
8:05	LONDON	ST2343	A2	ON TIME
8:15	MIAMI	HF3011	C3	DELAYED

ARRIVALS

TIME	TO	FLIGHT	GATE	REMARKS
8:35	FRANKFURT	ND1431	B4	ON TIME
8:40	SYDNEY	AC1047	B2	DELAYED
8:45	NEW YORK	NY1535	B1	ON TIME
8:55	BUENOS AIRES	AP5535	C1	ON TIME
9:05	ROME	HT3347	A3	ON TIME
9:15	CHICAGO	SF2113	--	------

Arrivals and departures

The big screens in the terminal list all the flights leaving and arriving today. Where's your plane going? Look for the departure time and the flight number. The screen will tell you which gate to use, and if your flight is on time.

check-in desk

Show your ticket and ID here to get a boarding pass, unless you have already downloaded one to your smartphone or tablet. You can take a small bag with you on the plane, but big ones are weighed here and given a special label to make sure they travel on the same flight as you. They are then sent off to the plane on a conveyor belt.

SECURITY CHECK

Flying by plane is one of the safest ways to travel. It's safer to fly than it is to take a train, car, or boat! Before you get on the plane, a lot of things need to be checked.

Bag Check

The small bag you take on the plane with you goes into the X-ray machine on a conveyor belt. It shines a special kind of wave through the bags and shows security staff what's inside. Here, staff will take away any items not allowed on the plane.

Identification

To fly by plane, grown-ups need special documents that prove who they are, such as an ID card or a driver's license. These are sometimes checked with electronic scanners. For traveling to another country, everyone needs a passport—a small book with details about you, plus your photograph.

Body scan

A special machine checks for metal on your body. Take off your belt, shoes, and jacket, and empty your pockets before entering the scanner, as any metal will make the alarm go off.

Pets and planes

In the past, animals weren't usually allowed on planes. Today, small pets come along sometimes. Guide dogs and other animals that do useful jobs are also allowed to travel on planes.

X-ray machine

As your hand luggage passes through the X-ray machine, the security staff look on the screen to see what's inside. They may ask to search your bag to make sure the contents are safe to take on the plane.

Pat down

If the alarm sounds, the security staff do a body search to make sure travelers aren't carrying anything dangerous. They sometimes use a handheld metal detector to find the item that set off the alarm.

BAGGAGE HANDLING

Remember the big bags you checked in at the desk? They now make their own journey to the plane. A sorter carousel makes sure each bag is sent to the right plane.

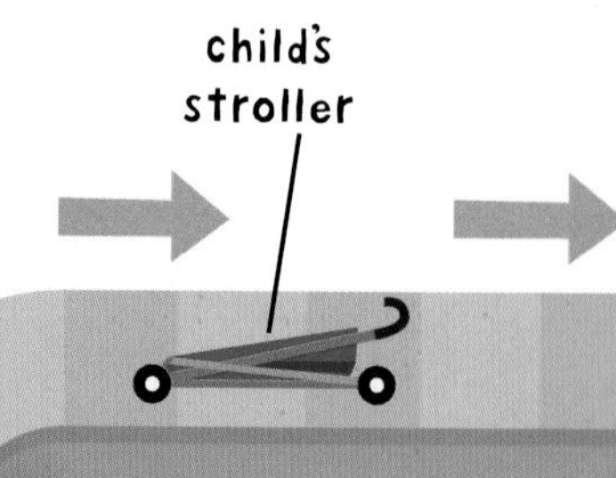

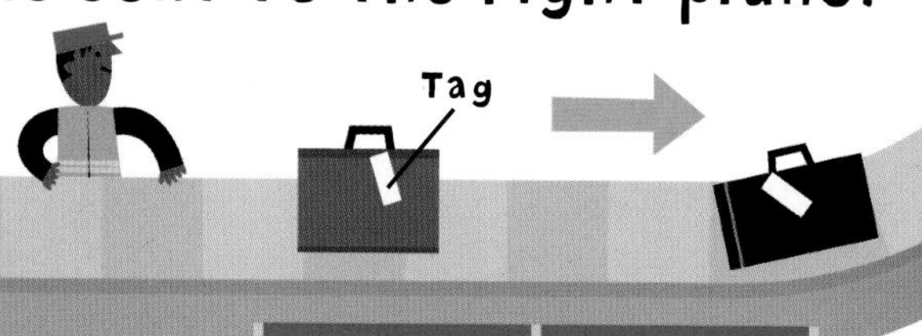

Tags

At check-in, each bag is given a tag that says which flight it is on. The bar code on the tag is scanned at specific points to keep track of the bag.

conveyor belt

A huge twisting and turning conveyor belt carries the bags from the check-in desk to the planes. The bigger the airport, the longer the belts. Some are many miles long, and carry millions of bags every year.

other items

Items that might easily break are loaded by hand. Larger items, such as bicycles or golf bags, have their own big carousel!

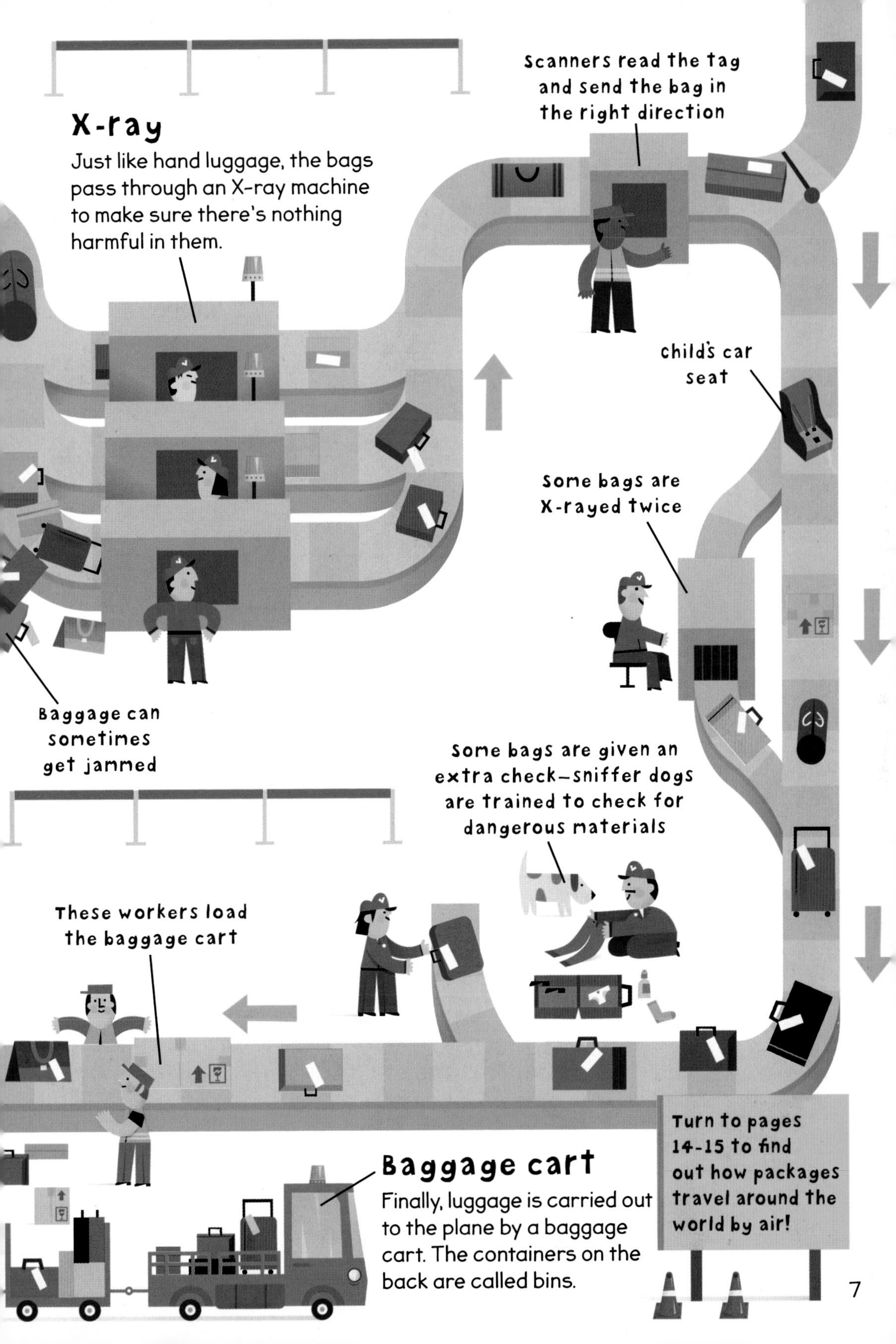

X-ray

Just like hand luggage, the bags pass through an X-ray machine to make sure there's nothing harmful in them.

Baggage cart

Finally, luggage is carried out to the plane by a baggage cart. The containers on the back are called bins.

Turn to pages 14-15 to find out how packages travel around the world by air!

PLANES AND OTHER VEHICLES

Airports are very busy places, where all sorts of aircraft are taking off and landing. Outside you can see passenger planes, private jets, and helicopters too!

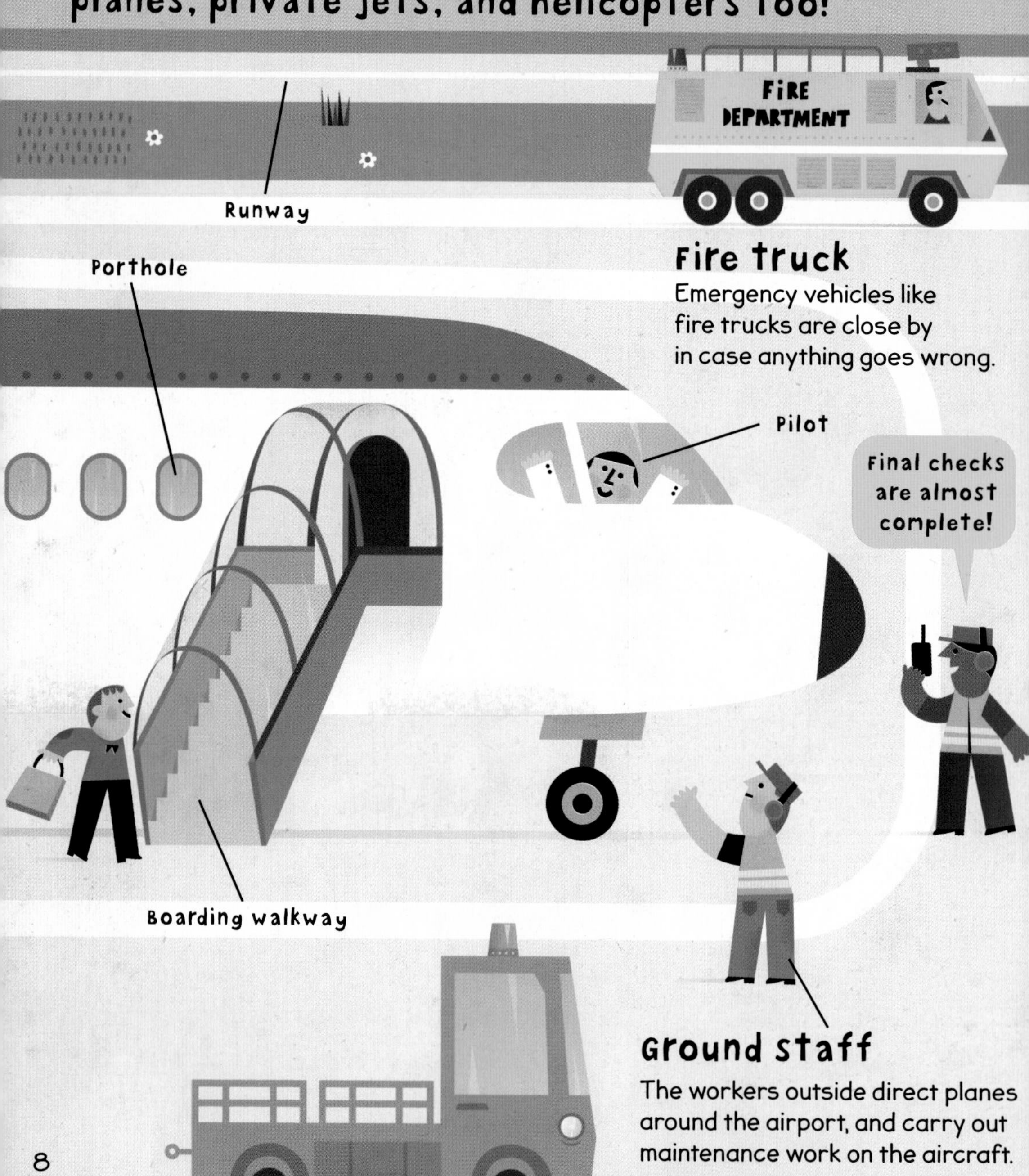

Fire truck

Emergency vehicles like fire trucks are close by in case anything goes wrong.

Ground staff

The workers outside direct planes around the airport, and carry out maintenance work on the aircraft.

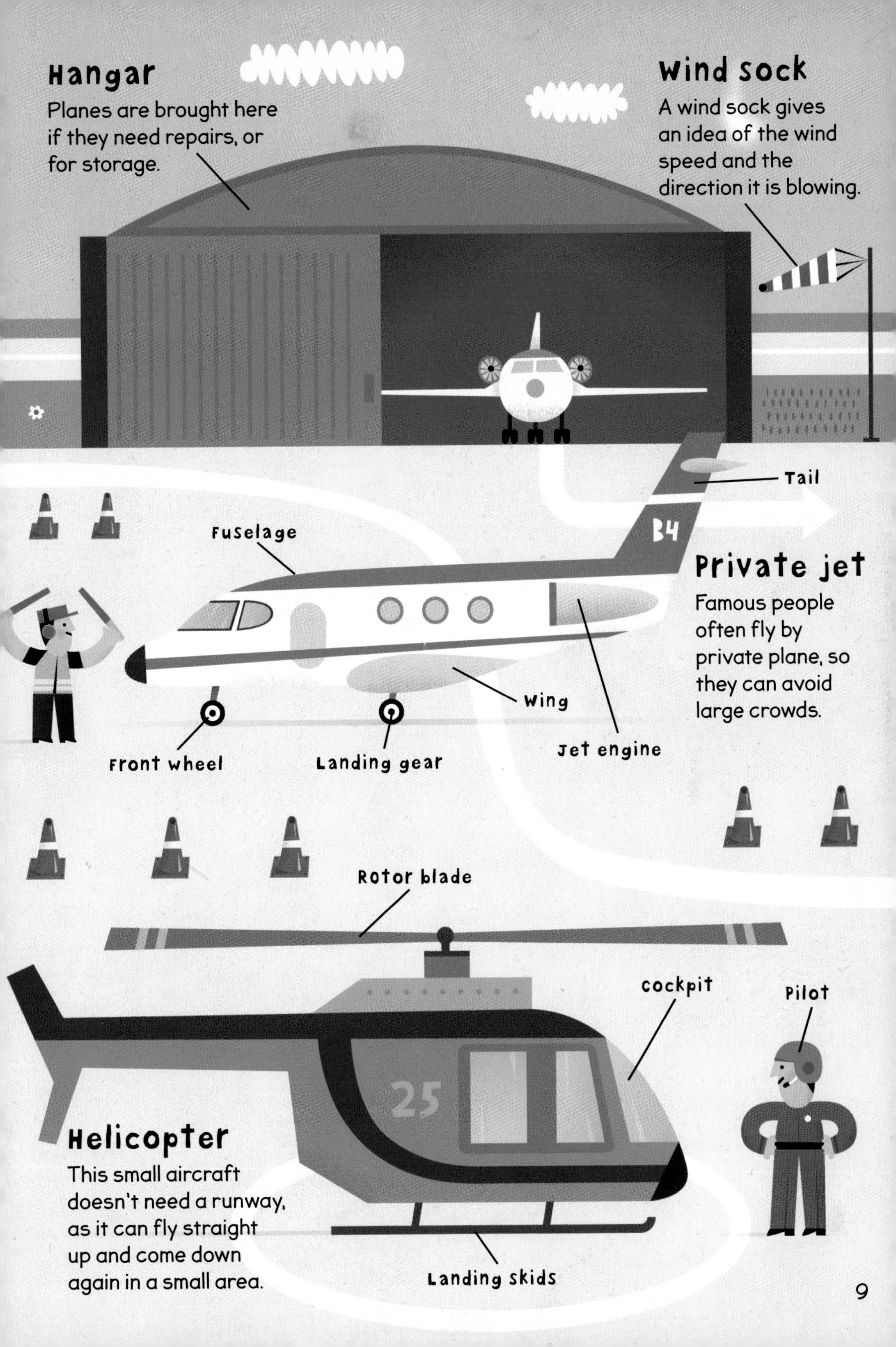
Hangar
Planes are brought here if they need repairs, or for storage.
Wind sock
A wind sock gives an idea of the wind speed and the direction it is blowing.
Tail
B4
Fuselage
Private jet
Famous people often fly by private plane, so they can avoid large crowds.
Wing
Jet engine
Front wheel
Landing gear
Rotor blade
Cockpit
Pilot
25
Helicopter
This small aircraft doesn't need a runway, as it can fly straight up and come down again in a small area.
Landing skids

THE DEPARTURE LOUNGE

While the crew and ground staff get the plane ready, you wait in the departure area. Here, you can eat, drink, shop, or relax until your plane is ready to board.

Moving walkway

Sometimes the departure gate is a long way away. But don't worry! Just stand on the moving walkway and it will take you to the gate!

Shopping area

Some of the shops here sell luxury items like watches and designer clothes. Other shops sell books, gifts, and souvenirs.

First and business class lounge

This quiet, relaxing area is for first class and business passengers. It has comfy chairs, food, and showers—ideal for those taking or arriving from long journeys.

computer screen shows which gate your plane is leaving from

Departure boards

These list all flights taking off from the airport. Keep an eye on them because they will tell you when it's time to go to your gate for boarding.

Gate

The staff at the gate check your passport and boarding pass, and then direct you to the plane.

Air bridge

You walk across this gangway to board your plane.

GETTING THE PLANE READY

Once a plane has landed and the passengers have disembarked, airport staff get it ready for the next flight. This is called "turnaround." The job takes many people and vehicles, and there is lots to do in very little time.

Apron

The area next to the departure gate is called the apron. Here, the plane picks up the passengers.

Baggage cart

These small trucks have bins that carry luggage from the airport to the plane.

Tug

A tow truck sometimes pulls the plane to the runway for takeoff.

Fuel truck

This vehicle has a huge tank that fills the plane with fuel.

Deicing truck

This vehicle services the engines to make sure they will work in cold weather.

Ground crew

These workers check the planes to make sure they're working properly. Before every flight, each plane goes through lots of checks to make sure everything is serviced and working correctly.

CARGO PLANES

Not all planes at airports carry passengers. Some carry goods, which are more commonly known as cargo. Cargo planes carry all sorts of things like food, cars, toys, furniture, and even zoo animals!

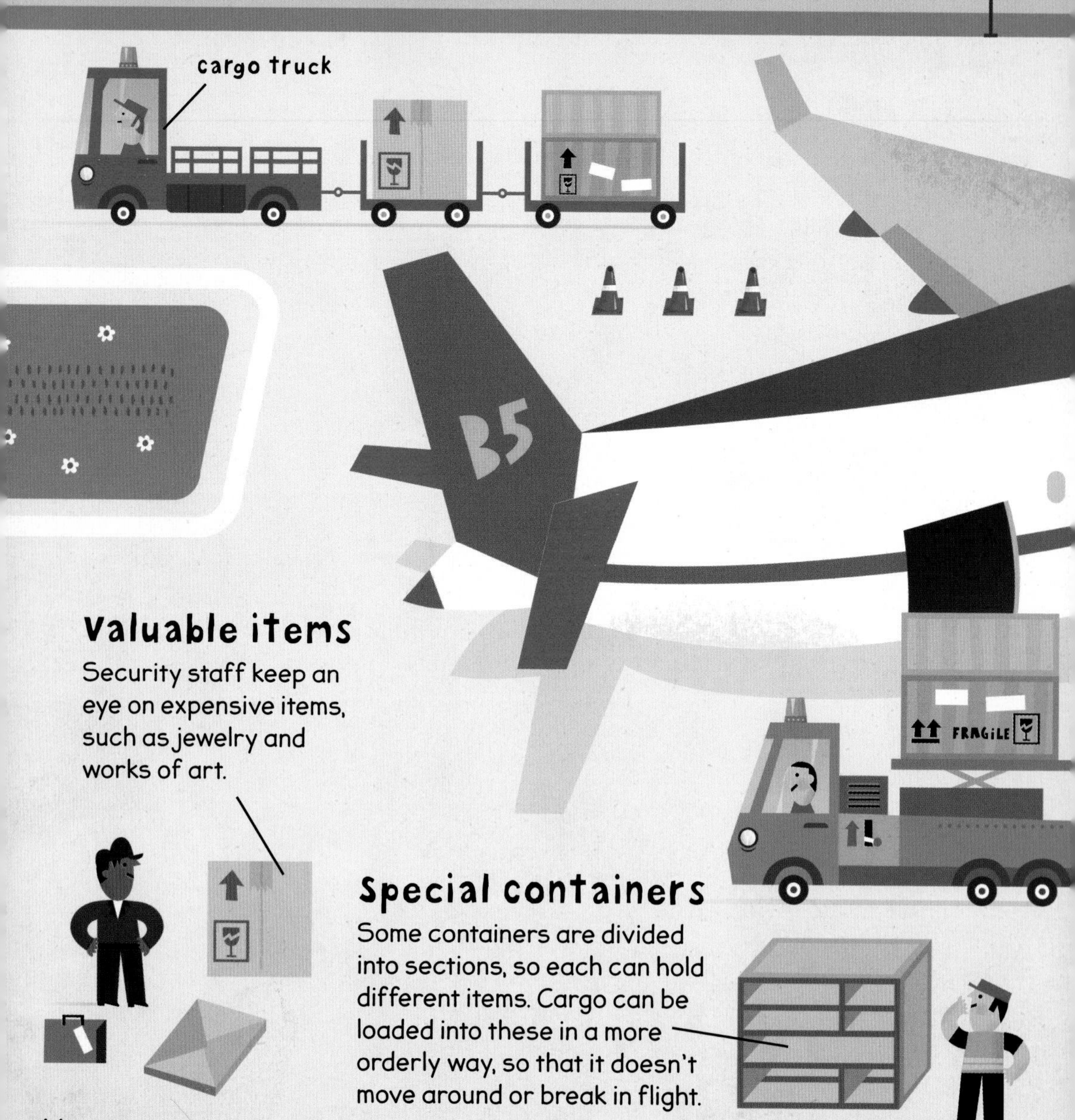

Valuable items

Security staff keep an eye on expensive items, such as jewelry and works of art.

Special containers

Some containers are divided into sections, so each can hold different items. Cargo can be loaded into these in a more orderly way, so that it doesn't move around or break in flight.

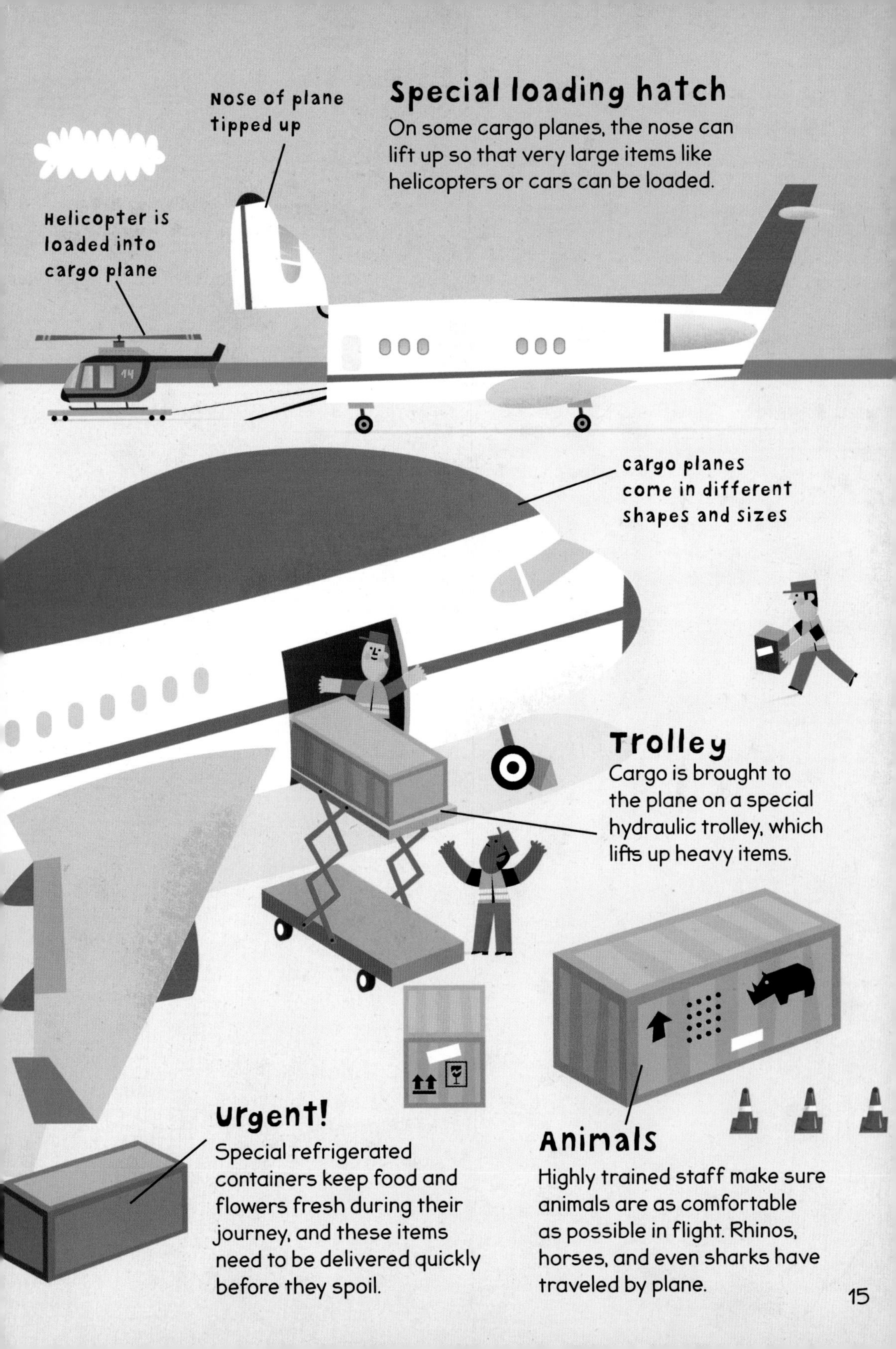

Special loading hatch

On some cargo planes, the nose can lift up so that very large items like helicopters or cars can be loaded.

Trolley

Cargo is brought to the plane on a special hydraulic trolley, which lifts up heavy items.

Urgent!

Special refrigerated containers keep food and flowers fresh during their journey, and these items need to be delivered quickly before they spoil.

Animals

Highly trained staff make sure animals are as comfortable as possible in flight. Rhinos, horses, and even sharks have traveled by plane.

AIR TRAFFIC CONTROL

Aircraft are taking off and landing at an airport around the clock. The air traffic controllers work inside a tower, and make sure the planes all come and go safely.

Air jam

At busy times, it's not possible for every plane to land right away. Instead, controllers ask pilots to fly around in circles until a space is cleared on the runway for them to land. An air traffic jam is called "stacking."

Planes stacking

Radar antenna

A radar antenna is a machine used to keep track of planes in the air. It sends out special waves, and when these waves bounce off a plane, a message is sent to the computers, telling the controller exactly where the plane is.

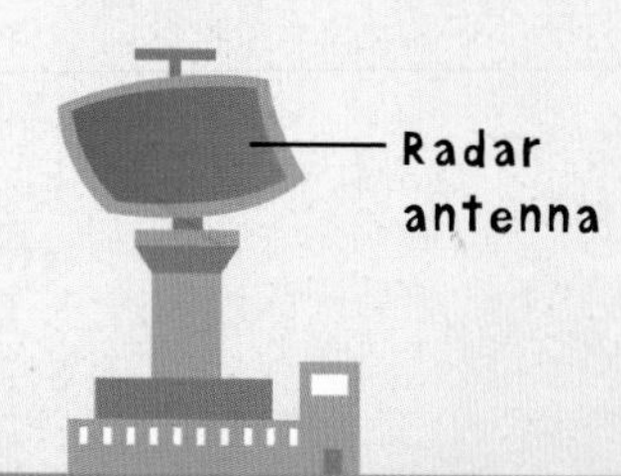

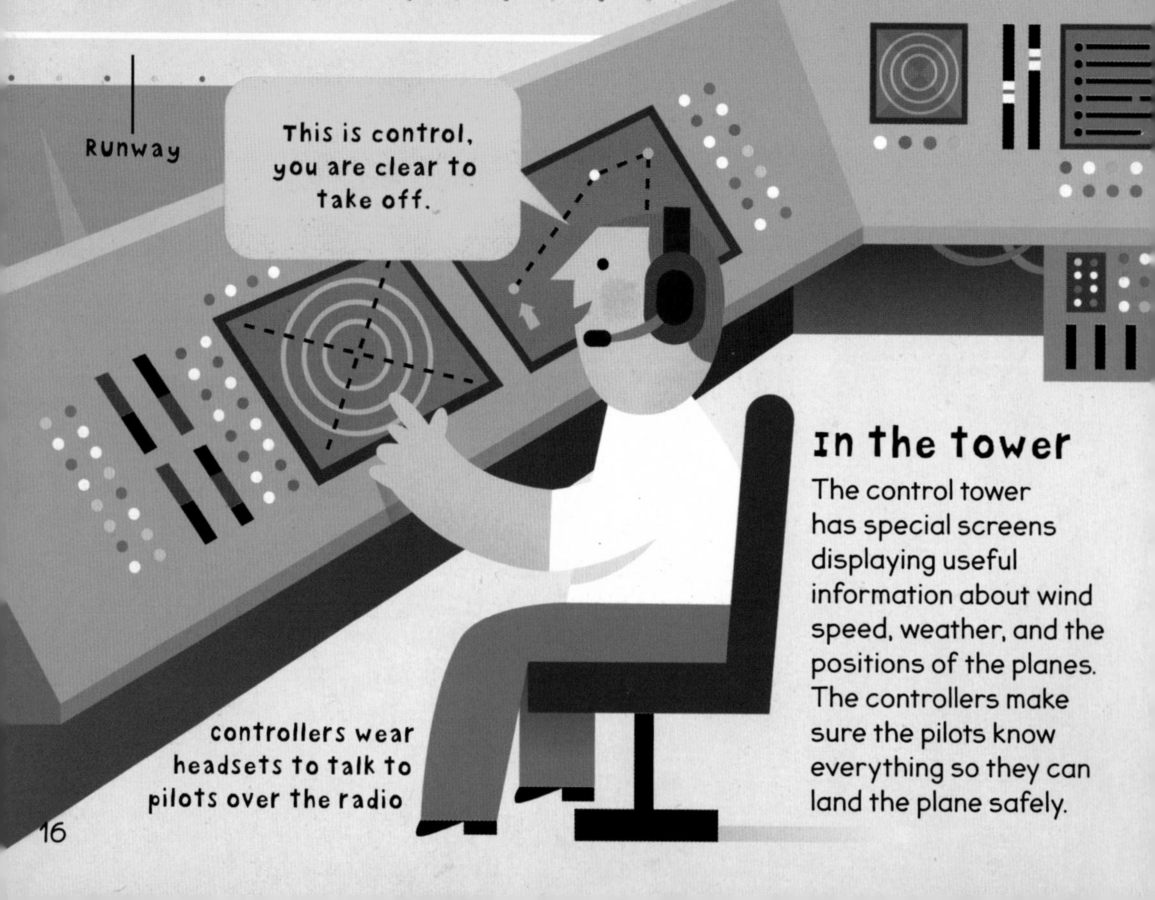

In the tower

The control tower has special screens displaying useful information about wind speed, weather, and the positions of the planes. The controllers make sure the pilots know everything so they can land the plane safely.

Controllers wear headsets to talk to pilots over the radio

control tower

Controllers usually work from a room in a tower. It has big glass windows so they can see every part of the airport.

computers

In the control room, the transponder signals are collected on a computer. The computer informs the controllers about the position of the plane.

working as a team

Controllers look after specific areas of the sky. Once your plane passes out of the area around the airport, another controller will be keeping an eye on it until you land safely at your destination.

START THE ENGINES!

when the seat belt light is on, you must put on your belt

Everyone is finally inside the plane, all the checks have been made, and you can't wait to get going. The plane moves away from the terminal and heads to the end of the runway, where it gets ready to take off.

Safety first

A cabin crew member will talk about safety before takeoff. They'll ask you to wear your seat belt, which will keep you secure in your seat, especially when the plane flies through a windy pocket of air that makes it bounce up and down.

controllers in the tower tell the pilots when they can take off

Takeoff!

Planes need to be moving very fast before they can fly. This means runways have to be long enough for planes to pick up plenty of speed. Most runways are at least two miles long!

Planes line up on the runway waiting for their turn to take off

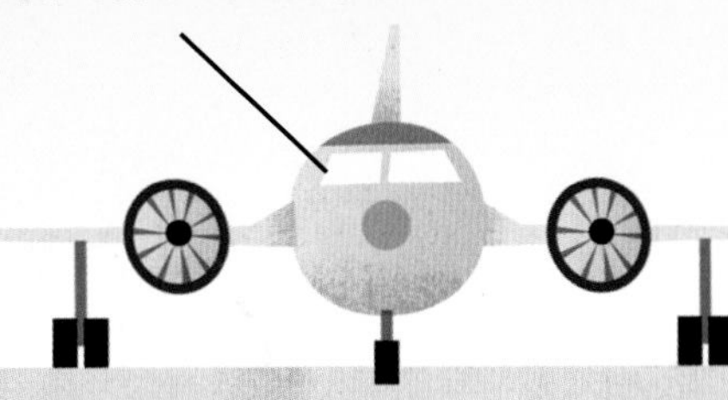

The cockpit

While you're settling into your seat in the cabin, the pilots in the cockpit are making their final checks.

Up, up, and away!

By the time the plane is ready to take off, it's speeding down the runway at about 180 miles per hour. That's when the pilot pulls back on the control column and the plane takes to the air.

IN FLIGHT

You're off on your adventure. So now that the plane is in the sky, what are some of the interesting things that happen on board as you travel toward your destination?

First and business class

This area of the plane has more space, and on longer flights the seats even turn into beds!

Cabin crew

The job of the cabin crew is to make sure you have everything you need for a safe and enjoyable flight.

Room for all

Some planes are quite small, with two rows of seats. Others, such as the Airbus A380, have seating on two levels, like a double-decker bus!

cart service

At mealtimes, the cabin crew will wheel a cart along the aisle to bring you a drink and food. Meals are prepared on the ground and then reheated in special ovens on board the plane.

In-flight entertainment

There may be a screen in front of you or overhead. You can choose to watch movies or TV shows on it, or maybe play games. There's even a map that shows you the location of your plane.

Window seat

If you have a seat next to the window, you can look out. You might be so high up that all you can see is blue sky with clouds below. It might not look like it, but you're traveling very fast—over 500 mph!

LANDING

Put your seat belt back on, it's time to land! You're nearly there. There's nothing more exciting than the moment your plane touches down on the runway.

Landing

As the plane nears the runway, the pilots lower the landing gear—big wheels that are safely tucked away inside the plane during the flight. The pilots line up the plane with the runway, lower the nose, and lift the wing flaps to slow the plane's speed. Finally, the wheels meet the ground. It's touchdown!

Arrival

Once you've landed, your plane may drive from the runway to the apron. This is called taxiing.

Transit bus

A transit bus carries people to the arrivals terminal if the plane is parked a long way away.

More traveling

Not everybody's journey is over when they land. Some people will be changing onto another plane to take them to their destination.

CARTS

Passport control

Before you're allowed into another country, officials will check your passport. Customs may check your bags to make sure you are not bringing anything that's not allowed.

Don't forget your bags!

The luggage you checked in at the beginning of your journey is now waiting to be collected. Screens will show you on which carousel you can find the bags from your flight. It's a good idea to decorate your bag with a bright tag or ribbon so you can find it easily.

ARRIVALS

You've arrived!

EXIT

You've reached the arrivals area. Is anyone here to meet you? This is where you will see them.

HOW TO ASSEMBLE YOUR MODELS

TERMINAL AND ROAD

❶ Open out the box and unfold the four road flaps.

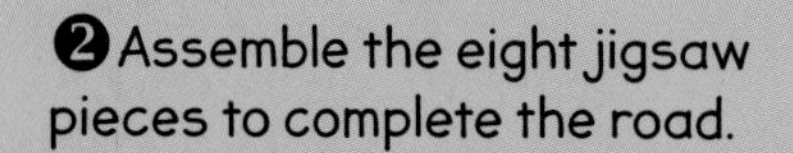

❷ Assemble the eight jigsaw pieces to complete the road.

CONTROL TOWER

Slot the two sections of the tower together until both sit flat at the base.

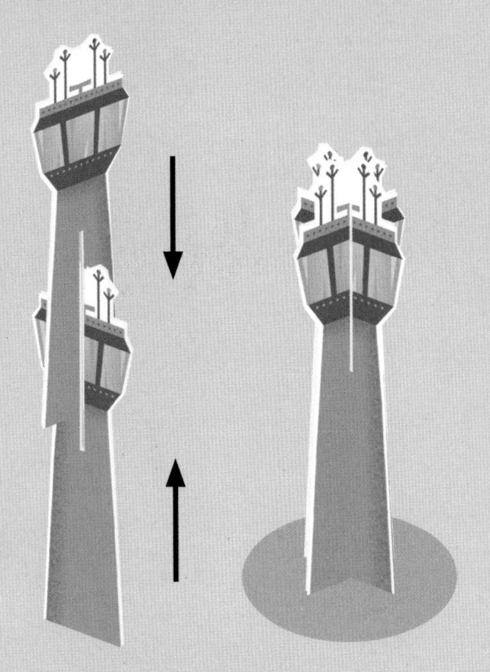

WIND SOCKS

Make the wind socks by slotting them into the base supports.

BAGGAGE TRUCK

Push the base support into the slot in the middle of the baggage truck.

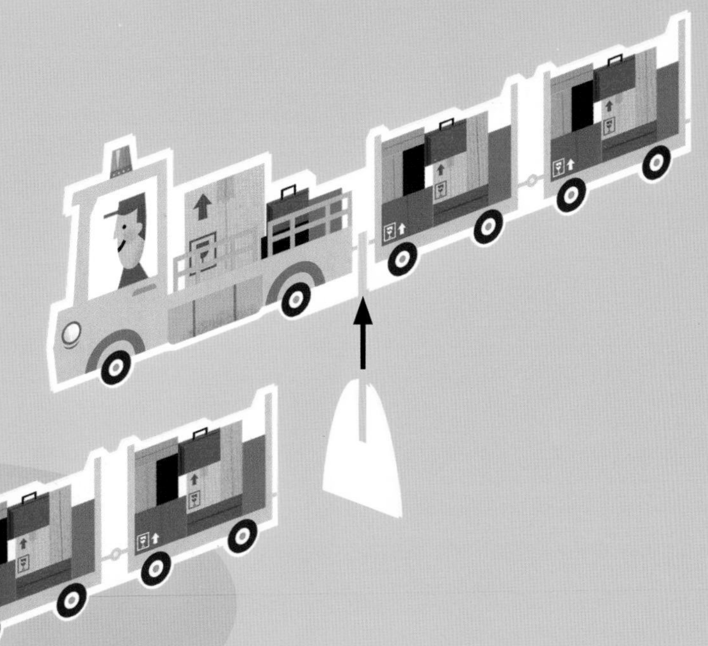

HELICOPTER AND CONTROLLERS

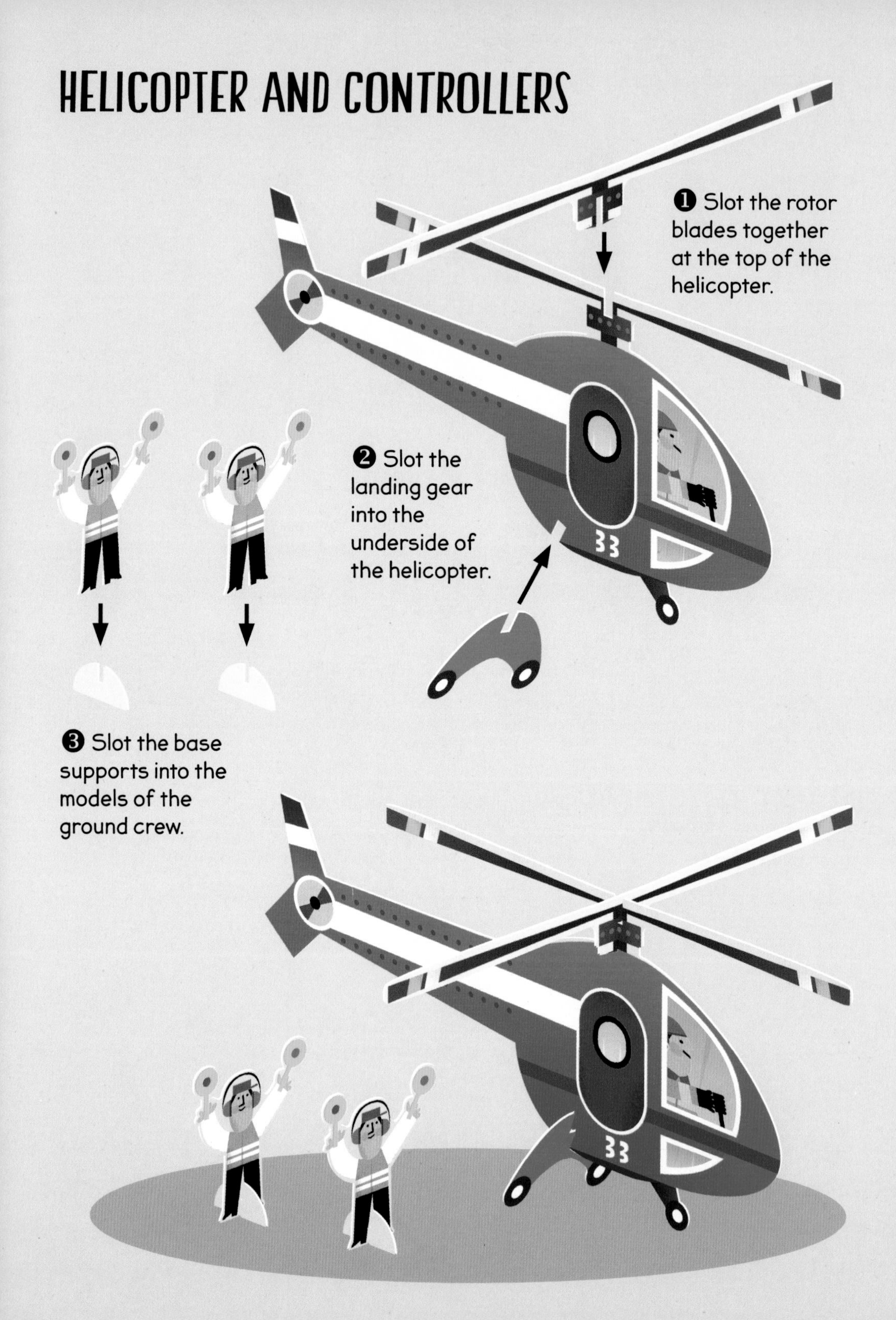

❶ Slot the rotor blades together at the top of the helicopter.

❷ Slot the landing gear into the underside of the helicopter.

❸ Slot the base supports into the models of the ground crew.

PASSENGER JET AND FUEL TRUCK

❶ Slot the wing piece through the fuselage so the wings are on both sides of the plane.

❷ Slot the engines and wheels into the front of the wings.

❸ Slot the tail into the back of the plane.

❹ Slot the fuel operator underneath the fueling vehicle.

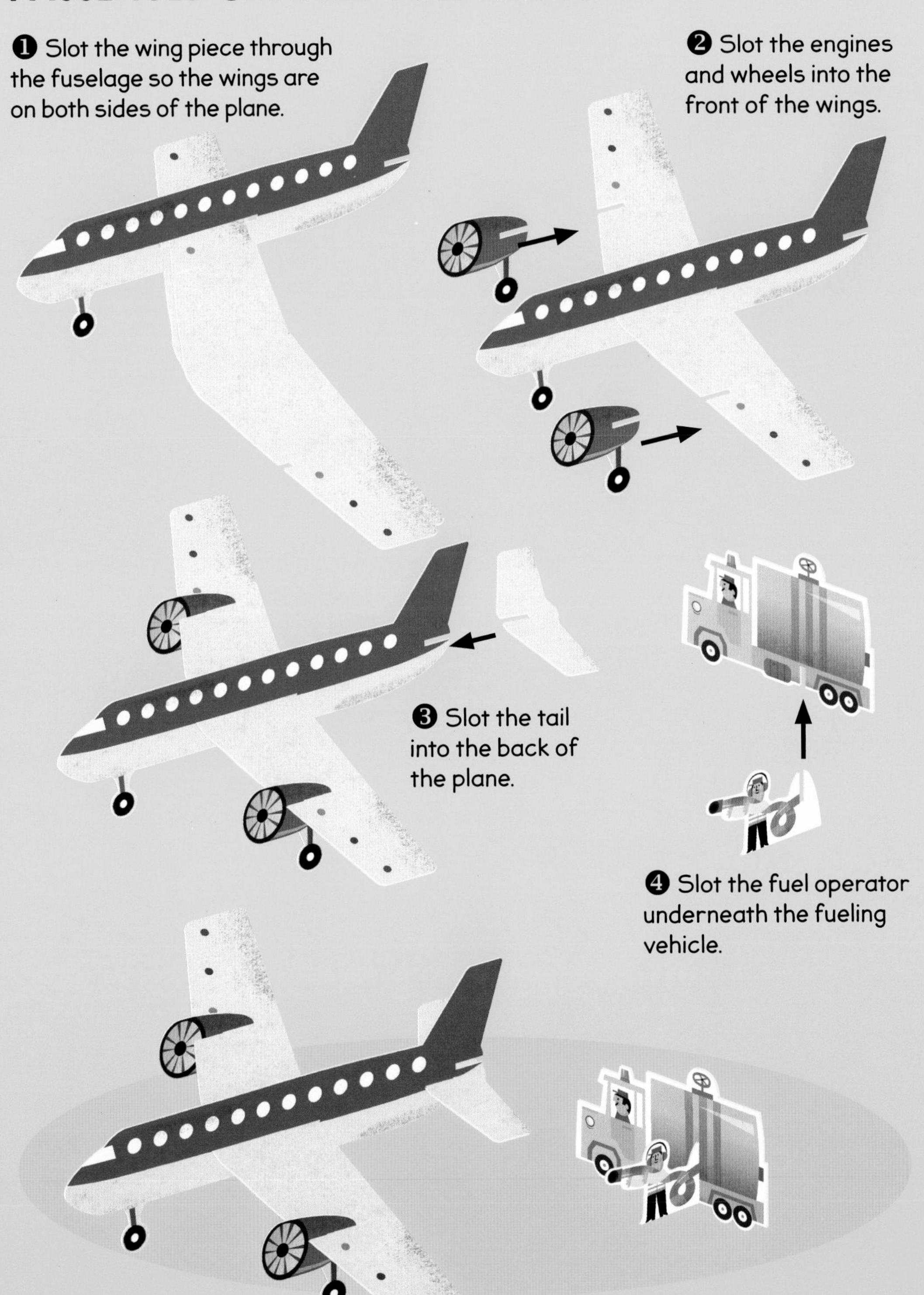

PRIVATE JET PLANE

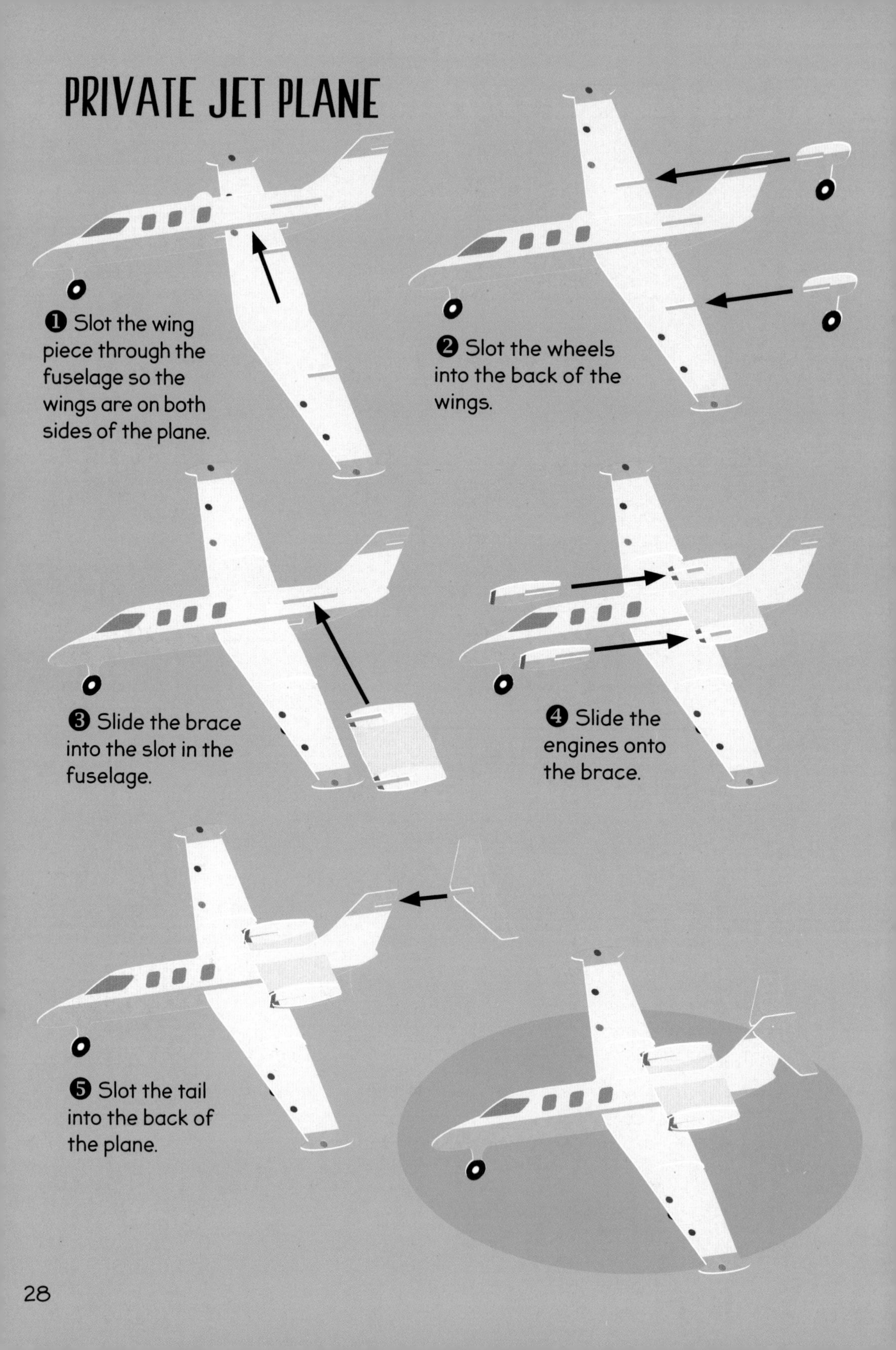

❶ Slot the wing piece through the fuselage so the wings are on both sides of the plane.

❷ Slot the wheels into the back of the wings.

❸ Slide the brace into the slot in the fuselage.

❹ Slide the engines onto the brace.

❺ Slot the tail into the back of the plane.

PROPELLER PLANE

❶ Slot the wing piece through the fuselage so the wings are on both sides of the plane.

❷ Slot the engines and wheels into the front of the wings.

❸ Slot the propellers into the fronts of the engines.

❹ Slot the tail into the back of the plane.

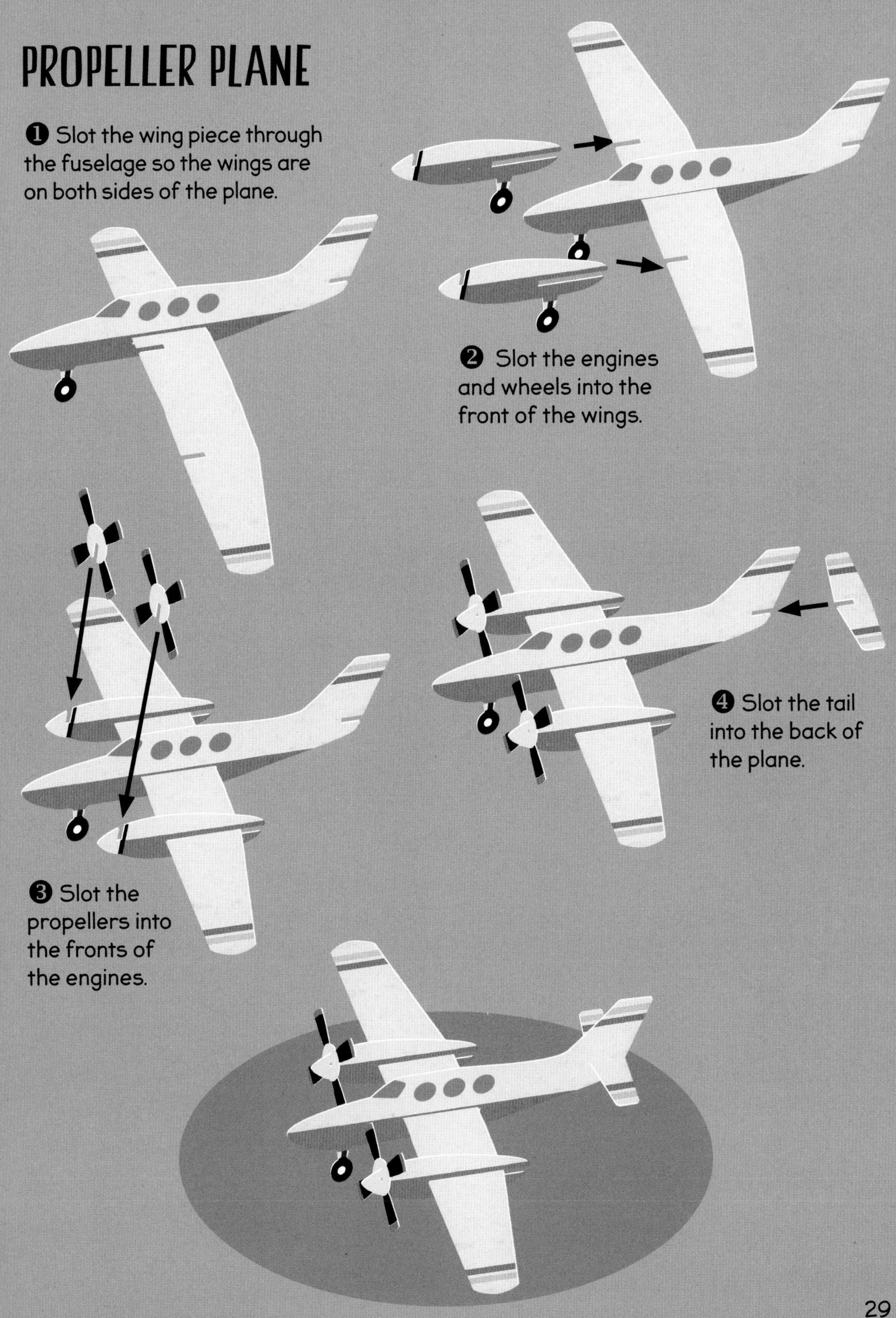

JUMBO JET AND BOARDING WALKWAY

❶ Slot the wing piece through the fuselage so the wings are on both sides of the plane.

❷ Slot the engines into the front of the wings. The two engine pieces with wheels go in the slots nearest to the fuselage.

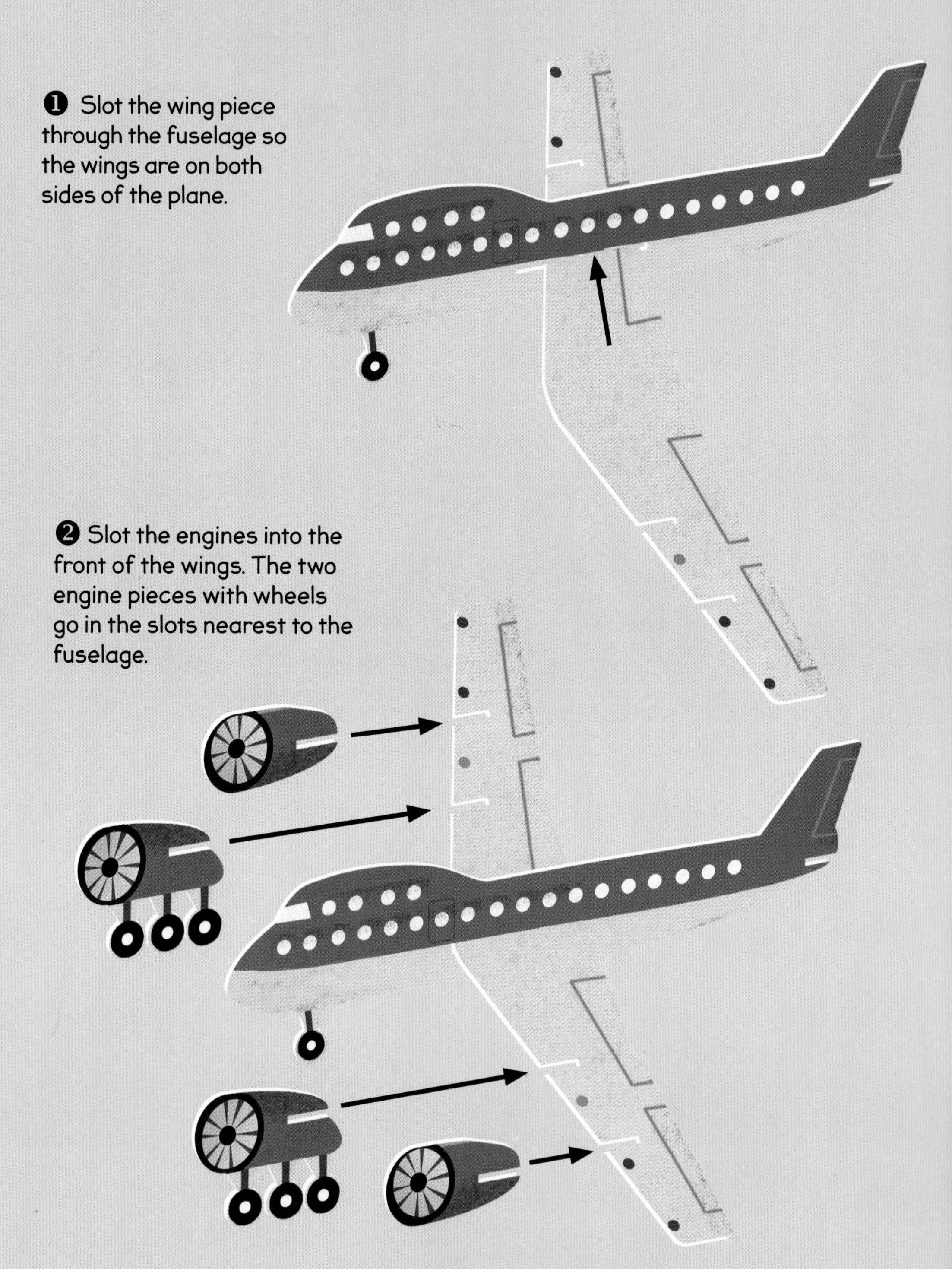

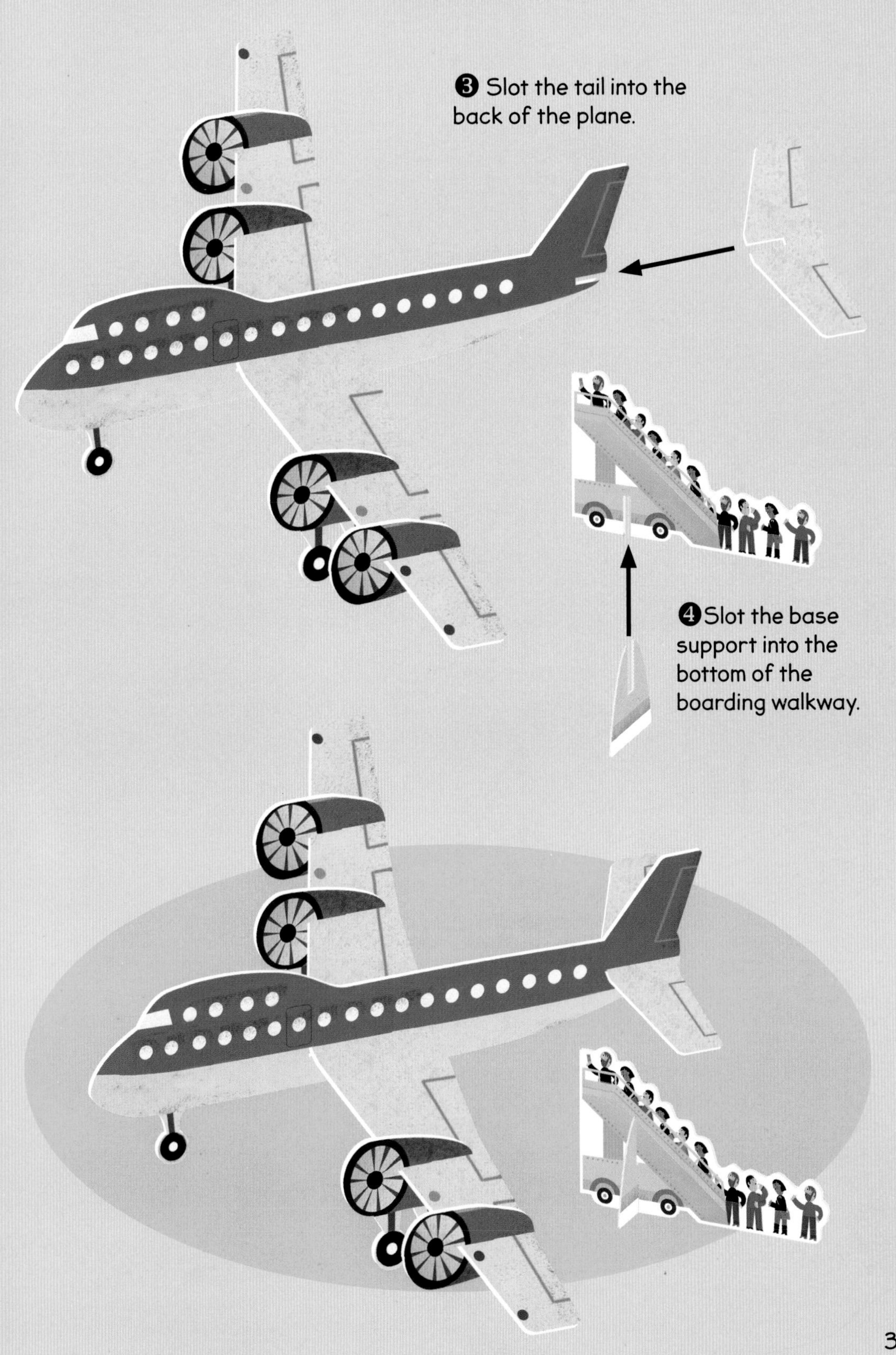
❸ Slot the tail into the back of the plane.
❹ Slot the base support into the bottom of the boarding walkway.

GLOSSARY

Airports are places specially designed for planes to land and take off with everything that passengers, crew, and the planes need for a smooth flight.

Air traffic control tower is a tall building with glass windows, where the controllers keep track of planes and make sure each one takes off and lands safely from the right runway and at the right time.

Arrivals is the part of the airport building you enter once you've taken off, or disembarked, the plane. It is also where people wait to meet and collect passengers.

Cabin crew is the team of people who work on the plane. During the flight, the crew makes sure you are safe and have everything you need.

Departure lounge is the place where you spend your time before boarding the plane. It has places to buy food and drinks, shops to pick up gifts and items you may have forgotten to pack, restrooms, and waiting areas with seats.

Departures is the area of the airport building you go through when you are taking a flight somewhere, or if you're dropping off passengers.

Ground staff are people who work outside the terminal, checking the planes after each flight, putting your luggage into the right plane, and making sure you get on it, too!

Hangars are giant garages, like a warehouse, where planes, helicopters, and other vehicles are parked overnight, or when they need servicing.

Passenger planes are aircraft that carry people around the world. They have lots of seats for people, and separate storage areas for their luggage.

Pilots are trained to fly a plane. Their training continues throughout their careers to make sure they are always prepared. Safety is important for all pilots.

Runways are long strips of concrete made specially for planes to take off from and land on. They have lights and lines to guide pilots to the ground.